About Skill Builders Subtraction

by R. B. Snow and Clareen Nelson-Arnold

Welcome to RBP Books' Skill Builders series. Like our Summer Bridge Activities collection, the Skill Builders series is designed to make learning both fun and rewarding.

Skill Builders Subtraction provides students with focused practice to help reinforce and develop subtraction skills. Each Skill Builders volume is grade-level appropriate with clear examples and instructions on each page to guide the lesson. In accordance with NCTM standards, exercises include a variety of activities to help students develop their ability to work with numbers in a subtraction format.

A critical thinking section includes exercises to develop higher-order thinking skills.

Learning is more effective when approached with an element of fun and enthusiasm—just as most children approach life. That's why the Skill Builders combine entertaining and academically sound exercises and fun themes to make reviewing basic skills fun and effective, for both you and your budding scholars.

© 2002, 2003, 2004 RBP Books
All rights reserved
www.summerbridgeactivities.com

Table of Contents

Number Writing Practice..... 3–4

Number Words 5

Counting................. 6

Greater and Fewer 7

Number Word Application ... 8–9

Writing Equations........... 10

Problem Solving 11–12

Story Problem 13

Equation Practice 14–15

Word Problem Solving 16

Subtraction Practice 17

Number Words 18

Word Problem Solving 19–21

Matching
   Equations and Answers 22

Multiple Choice
   Problem Solving 23–24

Equation Practice 25

Word Problem Solving 26

Problem Solving............ 27

Intensive Practice 28–29

Place Value:
   Tens and Ones 30–32

Number Word Practice....... 33

Counting................. 34

Problem Solving............ 35

Equation Practice 36

Problem Solving 37–38

Subtraction Picture.......... 39

Problem Solving............ 40

Equations 41

Money: Coin Value 42–43

Equations 44

Money: Counting Coins 45

Word Problem Solving 46

Problem Solving 47–49

Place Value:
   Tens and Ones 50

Two-Digit Subtraction......... 51

Critical Thinking:
   Math Investigations..... 52–65

Brain Teasers............ 66–74
   Looking for Patterns 66
   Maze 67
   Backwards Dot-to-Dot...... 68
   Problem Solving.......... 69
   Picture Problem 70–71
   Frog Follies.............. 72
   Color by Numbers 73
   Fishing Fables............ 74

Answer Pages 75–80

Number Writing Practice

Practice writing the numbers 0–5. Write a row of each.

0							
1							
2							
3							
4							
5							

Ah, numbers! One of my favorite things!

Number Writing Practice

Practice writing the numbers 6–10. Write a row of each.

6						
7						
8						
9						
10						

I'm growing a row of numbers.

Number Words

<u>Numeral</u> is another word for <u>number</u>. The following numerals and number words go together:

0—zero   1—one   2—two   3—three   4—four
5—five   6—six   7—seven   8—eight   9—nine
10—ten   11—eleven   12—twelve

Write the number word by each numeral.

5 **five**   6 _____

4 _____   12 _____

8 _____   7 _____

2 _____   0 _____

9 _____   1 _____

10 _____   6 _____

3 _____   11 _____

Counting

Write the missing numbers. Count backward.

20			17
	15		
		10	
			5
4			1

Greater and Fewer

Draw two fewer circles underneath each picture.

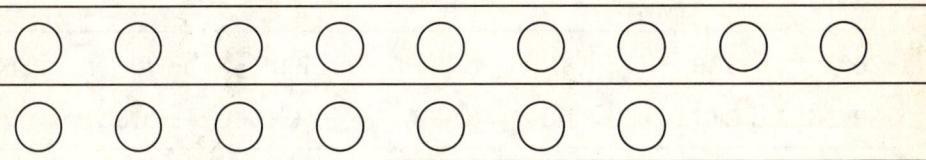

1. How many circles did you draw? _____7_____

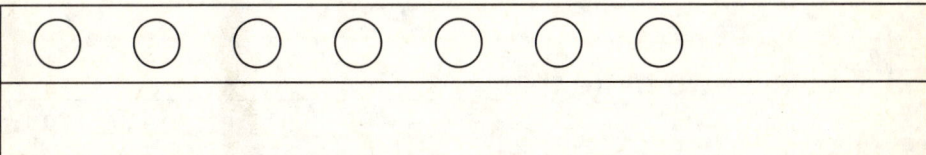

2. How many circles did you draw? _____

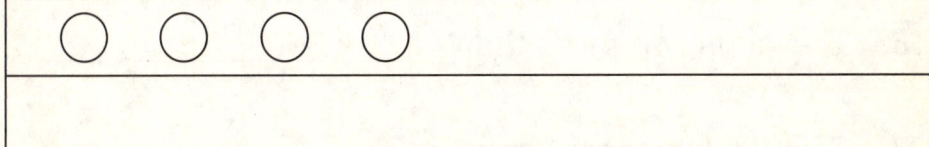

3. How many circles did you draw? _____

Number Word Application

Use the number words in the box to help you. Fill in each blank with a number word.

| 0-zero | 1-one | 2-two | 3-three | 4-four | 5-five | 6-six |
| 7-seven | 8-eight | 9-nine | 10-ten | 11-eleven | 12-twelve | |

1. Seven is one less than __**eight**__.

2. Twelve is one more than _____.

3. Five is two more than _____.

4. Ten comes before _____.

5. One is one less than _____.

6. Eleven is two more than _____.

7. Eight is two more than _____.

8. Zero is four less than _____.

9. Two is two more than _____.

10. Four is two less than _____.

Number Word Application

Use number words to answer the questions.

1. Three comes after _____**two**_____.

2. Seven is one less than _____.

3. Two comes between _____ and _____.

4. Twelve is one more than _____.

5. Zero comes before _____.

6. Eight comes between _____ and _____.

7. Nine comes after _____.

8. Five is two more than _____.

9. Ten comes before _____.

10. Four is one more than _____.

11. Eleven is two more than _____.

12. Ten is two less than _____.

13. Nine comes between _____ and _____.

14. Zero is four less than _____.

Writing Equations

Write a math sentence to go with each picture.

1.

   3 − __1__ = __2__

2.

   2 − ___ = ___

3.

   ___ − ___ = ___

4.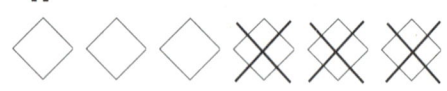

   ___ − ___ = ___

5.

   ___ − ___ = ___

6.

   ___ − ___ = ___

Problem Solving

Read the stories and write the difference.

1. There are 2 sailboats. 1 floats away. How many are left? 2 – 1 = __1__	2. There are 5 birds. 1 flies away. How many are left? 5 – 1 = _____

3. There were 3 pennies. 2 pennies got lost. How many are left?
 	
   3
 – 2
	4. There are 6 bananas. A monkey ate 2. Now how many bananas are there?
	
	   6
	 – 2

I lost some pennies... I wonder how much I have now.

Subtraction Grade 1—RBP3497

Problem Solving

Read the stories and write the difference.

1. There are 6 circles. ⊗ ⊗ ⊗ ⊗ ○ ○ Cross out 4. How many are not crossed out? 6 − 4 = **2**	2. There are 4 fish in a tank. No fish left the tank. How many fish are in the tank? 4 − 0 = _____
3. There are 6 rabbits. 1 hops away. How many are left? 6 − 1	4. There are 5 flowers. 2 get stepped on. How many are left? 5 − 2 = _____

Story Problem

Tanner and Lori were at the beach. They gathered seashells. All the seashells with the difference of 2 were broken. Solve the equations below. Color in the seashells that were not broken.

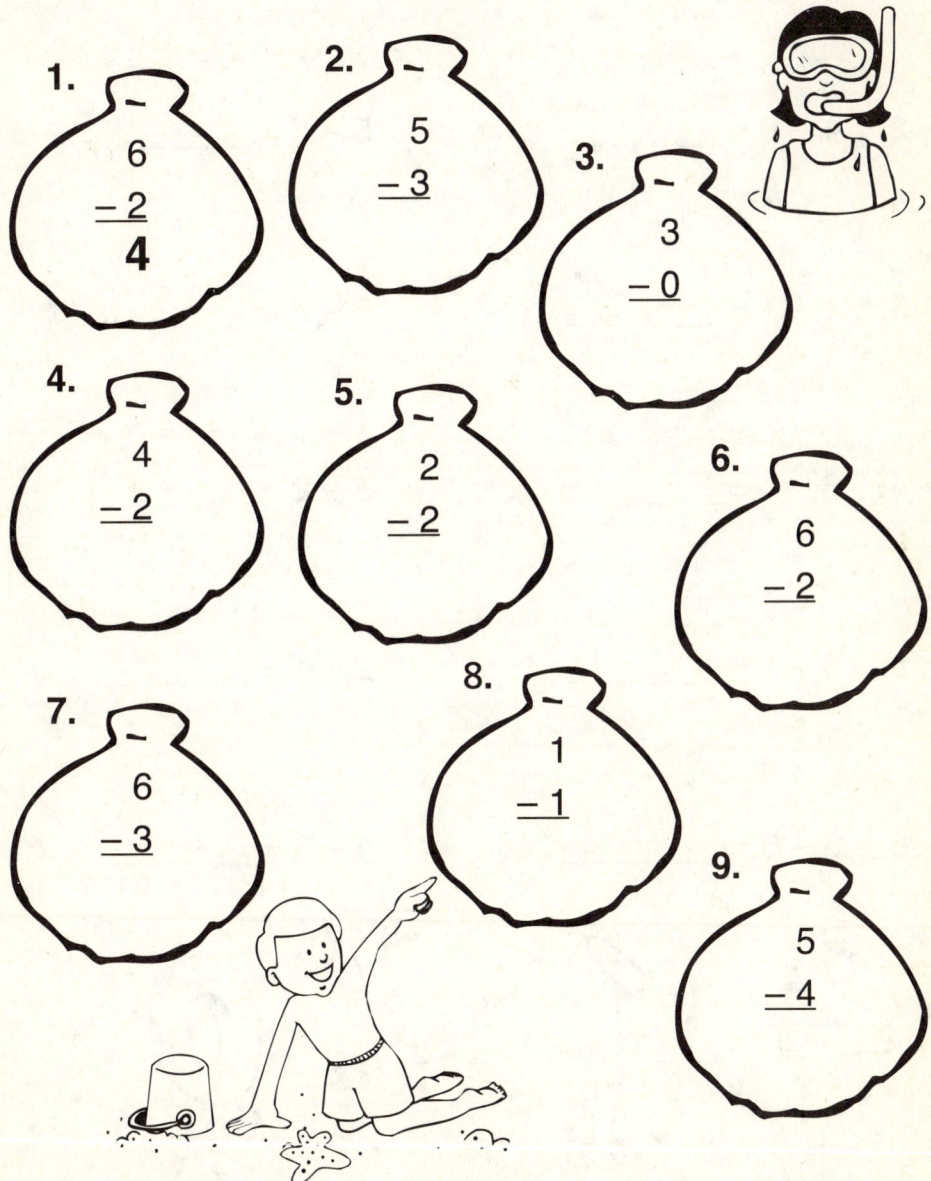

1. $6 - 2 = 4$
2. $5 - 3 =$
3. $3 - 0 =$
4. $4 - 2 =$
5. $2 - 2 =$
6. $6 - 2 =$
7. $6 - 3 =$
8. $1 - 1 =$
9. $5 - 4 =$

Equation Practice

Find each difference.

1. $1 - 0 = \underline{1}$ $2 - 0 = \underline{}$

2. $4 - 0 = \underline{}$ $5 - 5 = \underline{}$

3. $1 - 1 = \underline{}$ $2 - 2 = \underline{}$

4. $6 - 4 = \underline{}$ $5 - 2 = \underline{}$

5. $3 - 1 = \underline{}$ $2 - 1 = \underline{}$

6. $6 - 6 = \underline{}$ $4 - 3 = \underline{}$

Equation Practice

Find each difference.

1.
   $\begin{array}{r}6\\-2\\\hline 4\end{array}$ $\begin{array}{r}3\\-2\\\hline\end{array}$ $\begin{array}{r}5\\-5\\\hline\end{array}$ $\begin{array}{r}6\\-5\\\hline\end{array}$ $\begin{array}{r}5\\-3\\\hline\end{array}$

2.
   $\begin{array}{r}3\\-3\\\hline\end{array}$ $\begin{array}{r}4\\-1\\\hline\end{array}$ $\begin{array}{r}6\\-2\\\hline\end{array}$ $\begin{array}{r}5\\-4\\\hline\end{array}$ $\begin{array}{r}4\\-4\\\hline\end{array}$

3.
   $\begin{array}{r}6\\-0\\\hline\end{array}$ $\begin{array}{r}5\\-3\\\hline\end{array}$ $\begin{array}{r}1\\-1\\\hline\end{array}$ $\begin{array}{r}5\\-1\\\hline\end{array}$ $\begin{array}{r}3\\-0\\\hline\end{array}$

4.
   $\begin{array}{r}5\\-3\\\hline\end{array}$ $\begin{array}{r}6\\-1\\\hline\end{array}$ $\begin{array}{r}5\\-0\\\hline\end{array}$ $\begin{array}{r}6\\-3\\\hline\end{array}$ $\begin{array}{r}4\\-2\\\hline\end{array}$

Word Problem Solving

Read the story and answer the question.
Write the problem out on the lines.

1.	Tom had 2 worms for fishing. 1 worm got out of the can. How many worms are left? 2 – 1 = __1__	2.	6 stars were shining. A cloud covered 4 of them. How many stars are still shining? ___ – ___ = ___
3.	The dog had 6 bones. He did not eat any of them. How many bones does the dog have? ___ – ___ = ___	4.	Debra put 5 pennies in her bank. She took out 2 to buy a gum ball. How many pennies are in the bank now? ___ – ___ = ___

Must....not....eat....bones!
Must....not....eat....bones!
Must....not....

Subtraction Practice

Solve each problem.

1. $\begin{array}{r}5\\-3\\\hline 2\end{array}$ $\begin{array}{r}4\\-4\\\hline\end{array}$ $\begin{array}{r}2\\-1\\\hline\end{array}$ $\begin{array}{r}6\\-3\\\hline\end{array}$ $\begin{array}{r}5\\-1\\\hline\end{array}$

2. $\begin{array}{r}3\\-2\\\hline\end{array}$ $\begin{array}{r}4\\-0\\\hline\end{array}$ $\begin{array}{r}2\\-0\\\hline\end{array}$ $\begin{array}{r}5\\-5\\\hline\end{array}$ $\begin{array}{r}6\\-4\\\hline\end{array}$

3. $\begin{array}{r}6\\-6\\\hline\end{array}$ $\begin{array}{r}4\\-1\\\hline\end{array}$ $\begin{array}{r}3\\-2\\\hline\end{array}$ $\begin{array}{r}6\\-1\\\hline\end{array}$ $\begin{array}{r}4\\-0\\\hline\end{array}$

4. $\begin{array}{r}2\\-0\\\hline\end{array}$ $\begin{array}{r}0\\-0\\\hline\end{array}$ $\begin{array}{r}1\\-0\\\hline\end{array}$ $\begin{array}{r}6\\-2\\\hline\end{array}$ $\begin{array}{r}3\\-3\\\hline\end{array}$

5. $\begin{array}{r}4\\-2\\\hline\end{array}$ $\begin{array}{r}2\\-0\\\hline\end{array}$ $\begin{array}{r}4\\-1\\\hline\end{array}$ $\begin{array}{r}3\\-2\\\hline\end{array}$ $\begin{array}{r}3\\-0\\\hline\end{array}$

© RBP Books   Subtraction Grade 1—RBP3497

Number Words

Count the nuts. Draw a line from the number that tells how many nuts are shown to the matching number word. The first one is done for you.

1. 🥜 🥜 🥜 🥜		2. 🥜 🥜 🥜 🥜 🥜	
2	four	5	ten
3	five	8	five
④	two	10	seven
5	three	7	eight
3. 🥜 🥜 🥜		4. 🥜 🥜	
0	two	2	ten
3	one	9	eight
1	three	8	nine
2	zero	10	two

These math problems are making me hungry for peanut butter!

Word Problem Solving

Read the stories and solve the problem in the box.

1. Allie caught 4 fish. 1 fish jumped back in the ocean. How many fish did she have left?

   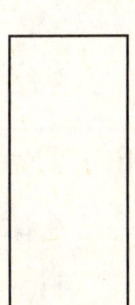

   ```
     4
   - 1
     3
   ```

2. 5 crabs are playing in the sand. 2 crabs crawl away. How many crabs are left?

3. 3 children are swimming. 2 get tired and go home. How many children stayed?

4. Tanner built 2 sand castles. 1 was washed away by the waves. How many sandcastles were left standing?

I'm feeling a bit crabby today!

Word Problem Solving

Count backwards to help you find the difference.

1.	There are 7 pennies. 4 roll away. How many are left? 7 – 4 = **3**	2.	There are 9 lollipops. 2 get eaten. How many are left? 9 – 2 = ____
3.	Mike has 11 books. He reads 5 books. How many does he have left to read? 11 – ____ = ____	4.	There are 8 fish. 3 swim away. How many are left? 8 – ____ = ____
5.	There were 10 shells. 5 were broken. How many were not broken? 10 – ____ = ____	6.	There are 12 boxes. 4 get thrown away. How many are not thrown away? 12 – ____ = ____

Word Problem Solving

Count backwards to help you find the difference.

1. There are 12 balls. 6 bounce away. How many are left?

    $$\begin{array}{r} 12 \\ -6 \\ \hline 6 \end{array}$$

2. There are 11 cups. 7 are used for hot chocolate. How many are not used?

3. There are 10 doughnuts. Dan eats 6. How many are left?

4. There are 12 eggs. Mom uses 2 for the cake. How many eggs are left?

Now Mom will never have to buy eggs again!

Matching Equations and Answers

Draw a line to the correct answer.

1.		2.	
9 − 1 = 7		11 − 4 = 3	
10 − 3 = 8		8 − 4 = 1	
11 − 9 = 3		12 − 9 = 7	
7 − 4 = 2		7 − 6 = 4	
3.		**4.**	
9 − 9 = 7		10 − 9 = 2	
11 − 6 = 2		8 − 6 = 1	
7 − 0 = 0		12 − 0 = 4	
12 − 10 = 5		11 − 7 = 12	
5.		**6.**	
7 − 2 = 2		10 − 4 = 6	
10 − 10 = 5		10 − 6 = 3	
12 − 3 = 0		8 − 5 = 9	
9 − 7 = 9		9 − 0 = 4	

Multiple Choice Problem Solving

Fill in the box by the correct answer.

1. $9 - 2 =$ 2 ☐ 9 ☐ 7 ■	2. $10 - 7 =$ 3 ☐ 4 ☐ 5 ☐	3. $7 - 5 =$ 6 ☐ 12 ☐ 2 ☐
4. $12 - 5 =$ 8 ☐ 7 ☐ 4 ☐	5. $11 - 9 =$ 2 ☐ 9 ☐ 3 ☐	6. $8 - 6 =$ 4 ☐ 3 ☐ 2 ☐
7. $12 - 3 =$ 9 ☐ 8 ☐ 6 ☐	8. $9 - 7 =$ 6 ☐ 4 ☐ 2 ☐	9. $11 - 2 =$ 6 ☐ 9 ☐ 3 ☐

Multiple Choice Problem Solving

Fill in the box by the correct answer.

1.
7 − 4 =
3 ■
2 ☐
1 ☐

2.
8 − 5 =
3 ☐
5 ☐
9 ☐

3.
12 − 8 =
6 ☐
5 ☐
4 ☐

4.
10 − 0 =
12 ☐
4 ☐
10 ☐

5.
10 − 10 =
10 ☐
9 ☐
0 ☐

6.
9 − 6 =
3 ☐
4 ☐
5 ☐

7.
12 − 9 =
9 ☐
6 ☐
3 ☐

8.
11 − 4 =
6 ☐
7 ☐
8 ☐

9.
8 − 2 =
6 ☐
8 ☐
5 ☐

Equation Practice

Complete the problems. Circle the problems that equal the number in the box.

1. **8**

   (10 − 2 = __8__)

   10 − 1 = ____

   11 − 3 = ____

   11 − 0 = ____

2. **10**

   11 − 1 = ____

   10 − 10 = ____

   10 − 0 = ____

   12 − 2 = ____

3. **4**

   2 − 2 = ____

   9 − 5 = ____

   11 − 7 = ____

   8 − 2 = ____

4. **5**

   11 − 6 = ____

   9 − 4 = ____

   7 − 2 = ____

   10 − 3 = ____

"We love this math stuff!"

Word Problem Solving

Read the story. Write a math sentence to solve the problem. Write the greater number first.

1. Mark has 12 pears in a basket. 4 of the pears are ripe. How many are not ripe?

    12 – 4 = __8__

2. Julie had 7 marbles in a bag. She lost 5 because the bag had a hole in it. How many marbles does she have?

    ____ – ____ = ____

3. Jim had 9 cookies in his lunch box. He gave 4 to his dad. How many cookies did Jim have left?

    ____ – ____ = ____

4. David had 12 books. He gave 6 books to Sam. How many did he have left?

    ____ – ____ = ____

5. There were 8 trees in my yard. I cut 2 down. How many trees do I have left?

    ____ – ____ = ____

6. Mr. Hobbs had 10 rows of carrots in his garden. 3 rows did not grow. How many rows did grow?

    ____ – ____ = ____

Problem Solving

A hermit crab has hidden under the object whose difference is three. Solve the problems to help Allie find the hermit crab. Color the crab's hiding place.

1. $\begin{array}{r} 7 \\ -2 \\ \hline 5 \end{array}$

2. $8 - 4 =$

3. $5 - 4 =$

4. $5 - 3 =$

5. $\begin{array}{r} 6 \\ -3 \\ \hline \end{array}$

6. $9 - 7 =$

Intensive Practice

Solve each problem below.

1.   8   9   12   10   7
      −4   −1   −12   −2   −4
       4

2.   12   9   11   7   12
      −6   −7   −7   −7   −3

3.   11   8   7   12   10
      −6   −3   −0   −7   −5

4.   11   10   11   10   10
      −5   −10   −9   −9   −3

I'm sure you'll have no problem finishing these problems!

Intensive Practice

Solve each problem below.

1.
10	7	11	12	8
− 6	− 6	− 0	− 10	− 6
4				

2.
8	12	11	9	7
− 5	− 0	− 2	− 3	− 1

3.
9	11	7	12	10
− 5	− 4	− 2	− 1	− 8

4.
12	12	8	10	10
− 8	− 5	− 1	− 1	− 4

I bet you can do these problems in a snap!

Place Value: Tens and Ones

Circle ten pennies in each group.
Write down how many you did not circle.

1. 1 ten __3__ ones

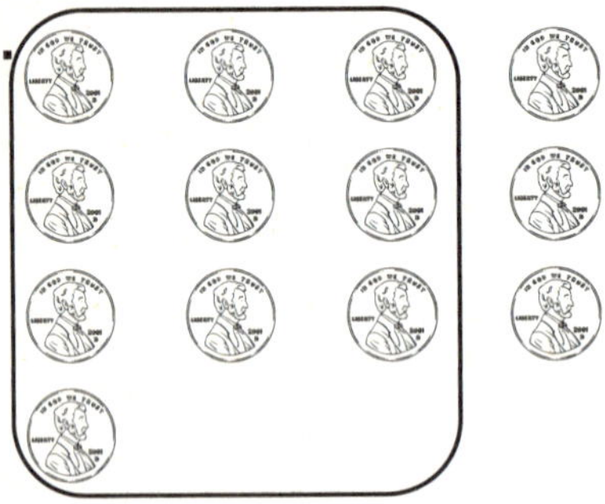

2. 1 ten _____ ones

3. 1 ten _____ ones

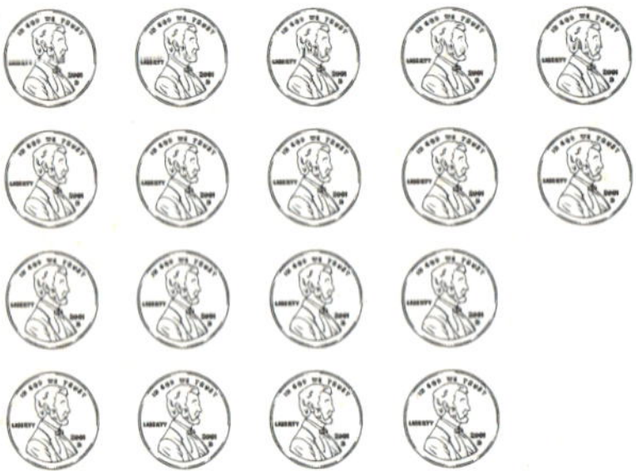

4. 1 ten _____ ones

Place Value: Tens and Ones

Circle ten pennies in each group.
Write down how many you did and did not circle.

1. __1__ ten __2__ ones

2. ____ ten ____ ones

3. ____ ten ____ ones

4. ____ ten ____ ones

Place Value: Tens and Ones

Circle ten pennies in each group.
Write down how many you did and did not circle.

1.

__1__ ten   __7__ ones

2.

____ ten   ____ ones

3.

____ ten   ____ ones

4.

____ ten   ____ ones

Number Word Practice

Write the numeral that is the same as the number word.

two __2__	three _____
ten _____	twelve _____
six _____	nine _____
zero _____	eight _____
four _____	eleven _____

Counting

Write the numeral that comes before each numeral listed.

1. **41**_42   ____10   ____96

2. ____31   ____38   ____20

3. ____40   ____18   ____14

4. ____66   ____16   ____90

5. ____80   ____ 7   ____27

Problem Solving

Count the shapes that are crossed off.
Subtract this amount from the total number of shapes to solve each problem.

1.
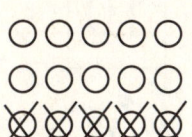
15 − **5** = **10**

2.
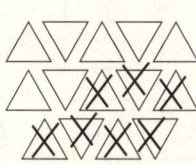
14 − ___ = ___

3.
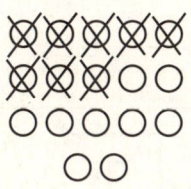
17 − ___ = ___

4.
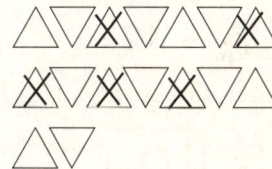
16 − ___ = ___

5. 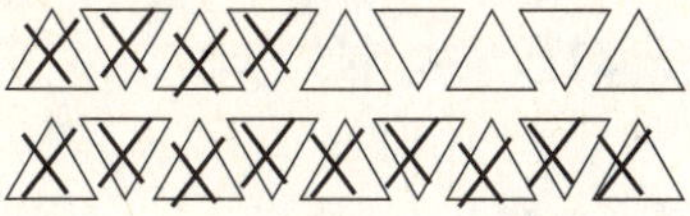
18 − ___ = ___

6. 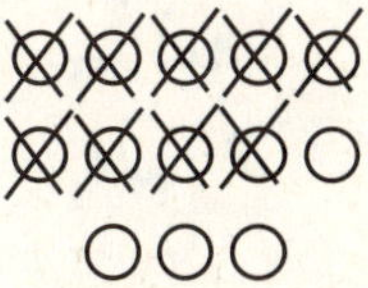
13 − ___ = ___

Equation Practice

Find the difference. Circle all the problems that equal the number in the box.

1. | 4 |

18 − 14 = 4
13 − 9 =
15 − 8 =
16 − 12 =

2. | 10 |

18 − 18 =
18 − 8 =
15 − 0 =
16 − 6 =

3. | 0 |

16 − 13 =
16 − 16 =
15 − 0 =
13 − 13 =

4. | 1 |

17 − 16 =
15 − 13 =
14 − 13 =
16 − 15 =

Problem Solving

Write the difference for each problem below.
Circle all the equations with a difference of 6.

1.
   - 16 − 4 = 12
   - 14 − 10
   - 13 − 3
   - 18 − 7
   - 15 − 8

2.
   - 14 − 14
   - 18 − 6
   - 17 − 5
   - 17 − 11
   - 14 − 8

3.
   - 13 − 7
   - 16 − 7
   - 13 − 0
   - 18 − 15
   - 18 − 18

4.
   - 15 − 9
   - 18 − 1
   - 13 − 5
   - 16 − 8
   - 15 − 3

5.
   - 13 − 6
   - 18 − 9
   - 18 − 0
   - 17 − 7
   - 14 − 3

Problem Solving

Write the difference for each problem below. Circle the equations in each row that have the same difference.

1.   15   13   17   18   18
      − 6   − 1   − 15   − 2   − 9
       9

2.   17   17   16   15   16
   − 11   − 3   − 0   − 9   − 13

3.   14   15   18   14   17
    − 9   − 4   − 13   − 2   − 10

4.   18   19   13   13   14
   − 10   − 6   − 0   − 9   − 13

5.   13   13   16   15   13
   − 10   − 12   − 15   − 12   − 8

Subtraction Picture

Write the differences. Color the picture using the coloring key below the picture.

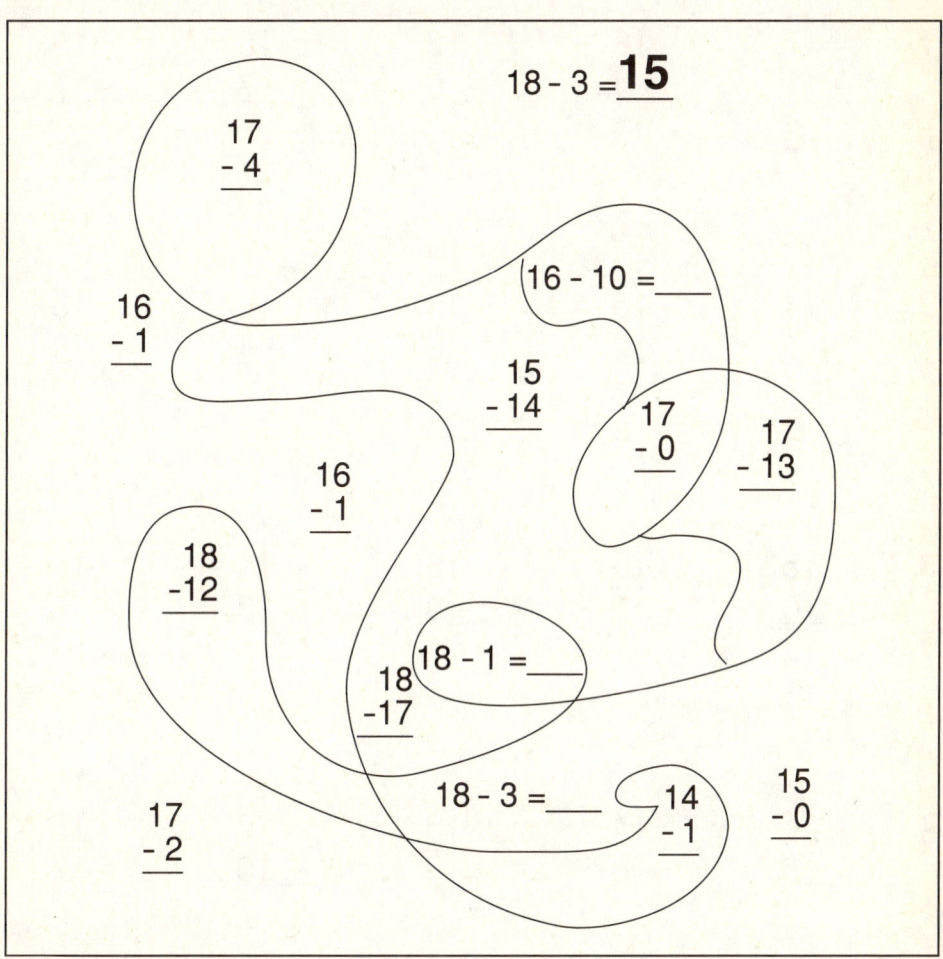

18 - 3 = **15**

17
- 4
___

16 - 10 = ___

16
- 1
___

15
- 14
___

17
- 0
___

17
- 13
___

16
- 1
___

18
-12
___

18
-17
___

18 - 1 = ___

17
- 2
___

18 - 3 = ___

14
- 1
___

15
- 0
___

Coloring Key

Where the answer is 17, color the space blue.
Where the answer is 6, color the space black.
Where the answer is 4, color the space orange.
Where the answer is 13, color the space red.
Where the answer is 1, color the space green.
Where the answer is 15, color the space yellow.

Problem Solving

Write each difference.

1.   17   18   13   16   15
      −11   − 4   − 5   − 7   −14
      6

2.   14   16   18   17   13
      − 6   − 10   − 9   − 4   − 10

3.   15   16   18   14   16
      − 10   − 11   − 8   − 13   − 16

4.   16   14   13   17   15
      − 8   − 8   − 8   − 10   − 7

5.   18   15   13   16   17
      − 6   − 9   − 2   − 6   − 12

Equations

Write each difference.

1. 14 − 9 = __5__ 16 − 9 = ____ 18 − 3 = ____ 15 − 8 = ____ 16 − 3 = ____	**2.** 16 − 4 = ____ 18 − 17 = ____ 17 − 9 = ____ 18 − 12 = ____ 17 − 15 = ____
3. 15 − 12 = ____ 14 − 7 = ____ 18 − 8 = ____ 14 − 0 = ____ 15 − 13 = ____	**4.** 13 − 1 = ____ 15 − 5 = ____ 16 − 4 = ____ 18 − 5 = ____ 14 − 11 = ____
5. 15 − 0 = ____ 18 − 11 = ____ 17 − 13 = ____ 14 − 10 = ____ 13 − 11 = ____	**6.** 18 − 1 = ____ 14 − 2 = ____ 16 − 1 = ____ 18 − 13 = ____ 16 − 14 = ____

Money: Coin Value

Use these money values to solve the problems on the next page.

A <u>penny</u> = 1¢.

A <u>nickel</u> = 5¢.

A <u>dime</u> = 10¢.

A <u>quarter</u> = 25¢.

I'm saving my money for a new basketball hoop!

Money: Coin Value

Solve the problems below. Draw the money if it will help you solve the problem.

1. 1 nickel = __5__ pennies.

2. 1 dime = _____ nickels.

3. 1 quarter = _____ nickels.

4. 1 dime – 1 nickel = _____ pennies.

5. 4 nickels = _____ dimes.

6. 1 quarter = _____ dimes and _____ nickel.

Equations

Write each difference.

1. 13 − 3 = __10__
   15 − 1 = _____
   16 − 12 = _____
   17 − 14 = _____
   18 − 0 = _____

2. 13 − 12 = _____
   16 − 0 = _____
   18 − 2 = _____
   17 − 5 = _____
   18 − 4 = _____

3. 14 − 1 = _____
   13 − 13 = _____
   16 − 2 = _____
   18 − 2 = _____
   17 − 16 = _____

4. 14 − 3 = _____
   15 − 2 = _____
   17 − 1 = _____
   14 − 12 = _____
   15 − 15 = _____

5. 17 − 17 = _____
   15 − 3 = _____
   14 − 14 = _____
   17 − 6 = _____
   15 − 14 = _____

6. 14 − 12 = _____
   15 − 4 = _____
   17 − 2 = _____
   16 − 7 = _____
   17 − 0 = _____

Money: Counting Coins

Count the coins.
Write the total amount of money they make.

1.

_____8_____ ¢

2.

_____ ¢

3.

_____ ¢

4.

_____ ¢

Ummmm, do I have enough?

Pens 35¢

Word Problem Solving

Read the stories. Solve the problems.

1. Tom had 18¢.
   He spent 9¢.
   How much does he have left?

   18¢ – 9¢ = 9¢

2. Mary had 15¢.
   She lost 4¢.
   How much does she have left?

   ___ – ___ = ___

3. Brittany had 16 pennies. She gave 8 of them to Joe. How many pennies does she have left?

   ___ – ___ = ___

4. Emily had 17¢.
   She put 9¢ in her bank. How much did she have left?

   ___ – ___ = ___

I'm saving my money for summer vacation!

Problem Solving

Write each difference.

1.
   12　　　 8　　　 11　　　 6　　　 3
  −10　　 −7　　 −10　　 −4　　 −2
   2

2.
    7　　　 14　　　 4　　　 10　　　 8
   −5　　 −7　　 −3　　 −9　　 −8

3.
    9　　　 12　　　 2　　　 6　　　 13
   −8　　 −2　　 −0　　 −1　　 −6

4.
    5　　　 10　　　 8　　　 7　　　 5
   −2　　 −10　　 −5　　 −3　　 −5

5.
    6　　　 12　　　 9　　　 17　　　 9
   −3　　 −4　　 −6　　 −8　　 −9

More Problem Solving

Write each difference.

1. 6 – 5 = __1__

   4 – 4 = ____

   10 – 6 = ____

   9 – 3 = ____

   7 – 7 = ____

2. 8 – 3 = ____

   7 – 2 = ____

   12 – 1 = ____

   9 – 7 = ____

   6 – 2 = ____

3. 3 – 3 = ____

   18 – 10 = ____

   14 – 6 = ____

   9 – 5 = ____

   8 – 4 = ____

4. 12 – 9 = ____

   7 – 6 = ____

   14 – 10 = ____

   13 – 9 = ____

   10 – 3 = ____

Good job! You didn't even have to take off your shoes!

More Problem Solving

Write each difference.

1.   6 − 0 = __6__

    13 − 11 = _____

    16 − 4 = _____

    1 − 1 = _____

2.   0 − 0 = _____

    12 − 8 = _____

    15 − 2 = _____

    9 − 1 = _____

3.   5 − 3 = _____

    1 − 0 = _____

    12 − 7 = _____

    7 − 1 = _____

4.   15 − 9 = _____

    17 − 14 = _____

    11 − 8 = _____

    5 − 4 = _____

5.   5 − 1 = _____

    18 − 4 = _____

    9 − 4 = _____

    11 − 2 = _____

Phew! I'm glad we're done with those problems!

Place Value: Tens and Ones

Read carefully and fill in the blanks.

1. 74 = __7__ tens __4__ ones
2. 96 = _____ tens _____ ones
3. 4 tens 3 ones = _____
4. 7 tens 8 ones = _____
5. 10 tens 0 ones = _____
6. 33 = _____ tens _____ ones
7. 50 = _____ tens _____ ones
8. 2 tens 6 ones = _____
9. 5 tens 2 ones = _____
10. 38 = _____ tens _____ ones
11. 49 = _____ tens _____ ones
12. 6 tens 6 ones = _____
13. 3 tens 5 ones = _____
14. 100 = _____ tens _____ ones

Two-Digit Subtraction

Solve the problems below.

1.
   48   38   27   32   86
− 22   − 11   − 16   − 12   − 66
   26

2.
   30   19   67   44   89
− 30   − 17   − 42   − 22   − 63

3.
   99   24   51   88   67
− 30   − 24   − 40   − 11   − 22

4.
   63   49   87   40   82
− 53   − 21   − 63   − 10   − 11

5.
   45   51   36   38   75
− 23   − 30   − 12   − 31   − 42

Critical Thinking Skills

Math Investigations

Complete the problems to solve the puzzle.

Across

1. 20 − 9 = _____
3. 17 − 5 = _____
5. 62 − 20 = _____
8. 16 − 3 = _____
10. 93 − 30 = _____
12. 75 − 30 = _____
14. 30 − 10 = _____

Down

2. 19 − 5 = _____
4. 50 − 25 = _____
6. 21 − 0 = _____
7. 18 − 2 = _____
9. 84 − 50 = _____
11. 42 − 10 = _____
13. 100 − 50 = _____

Math Investigations

Match the picture to the number sentence. Complete the number sentence.

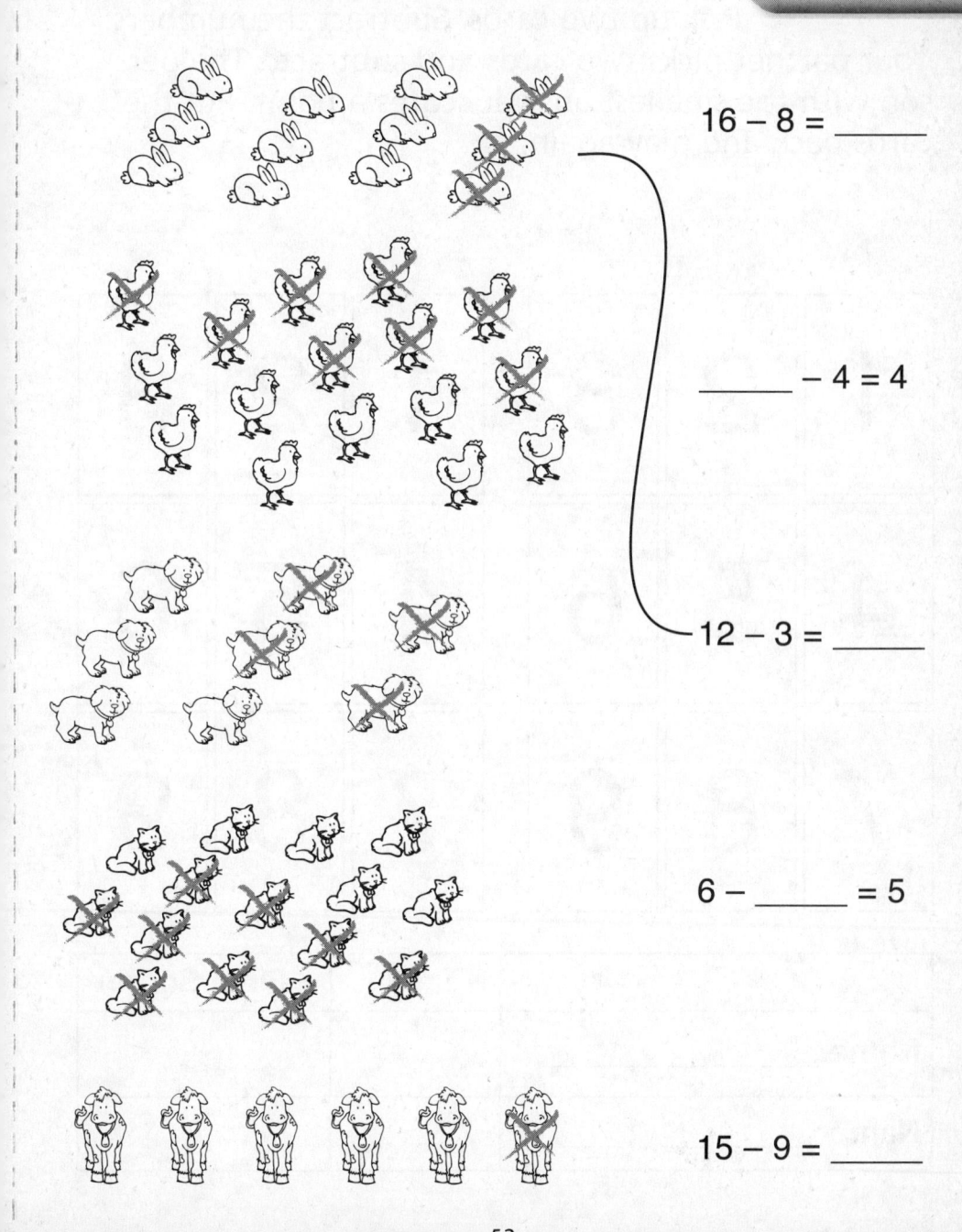

Critical Thinking Skills

16 − 8 = _____

_____ − 4 = 4

12 − 3 = _____

6 − _____ = 5

15 − 9 = _____

Critical Thinking Skills

Math Investigations

Enlarge and copy this page. Cut out the cards. Turn them over and mix them up. Pick up two cards. Subtract the numbers. Your partner picks two cards and subtracts. The person with the smallest answer scores a point. Put the cards back and play again.

1	2	3		1	2	3
4	5	6		4	5	6
7	8	9		7	8	9

	Tally	Final Score
Name _____		
Name _____		

Math Investigations

Help James and John find their cat. Look for tens and ones in backward order from 20 to 10. Draw a path.

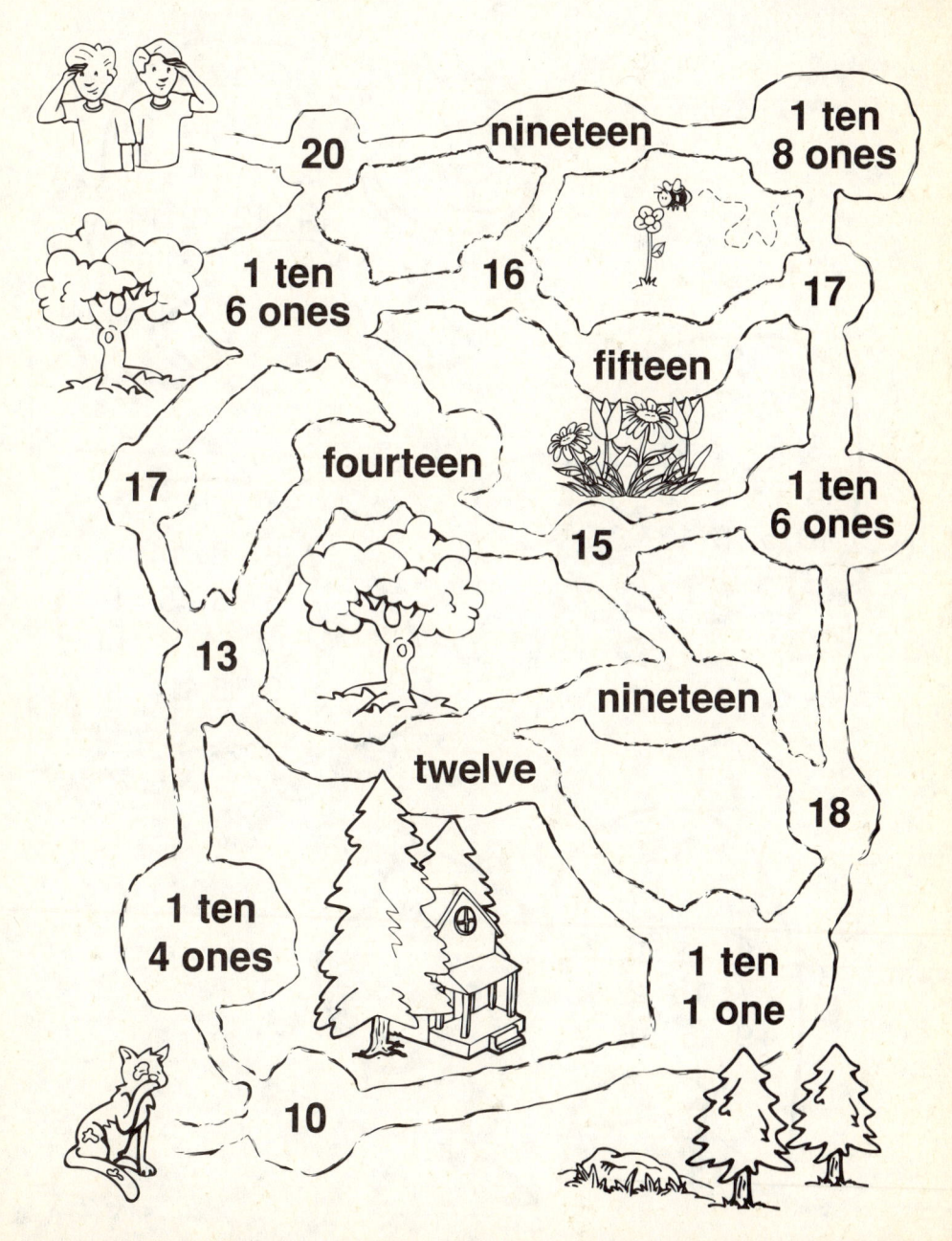

Critical Thinking Skills

20 — nineteen — 1 ten 8 ones

1 ten 6 ones — 16 — 17

17 — fourteen — fifteen — 1 ten 6 ones

13 — 15 — nineteen — 18

1 ten 4 ones — twelve — 1 ten 1 one

10

55

© RBP Books

Subtraction Grade 1—RBP3497

Critical Thinking Skills

Math Investigations

Find the families of facts in the animals and circle them.

12
6 8 14 8
2 6 4 5
4 12 12 14
(9 3 12) 9

13
13 6 7 9
8 7 2 2
5 13 6 13
13 5 8 13

14
6 8 14 9
8 8 5 5
14 14 6 14
9 5 14 9

15
15 5 10 9
4 3 6 6
7 15 2 15
9 6 15 2

Math Investigations

Critical Thinking Skills

Subtract to show how many are left.

1. $11 - 3 = \square\ - 4 = \square\ - 2 = \square$

2. $13 - 4 = \square\ - 3 = \square\ - 1 = \square$

3. $15 - 2 = \square\ - 8 = \square\ - 3 = \square$

4. $16 - 8 = \square\ - 2 = \square\ - 1 = \square$

5. $10 - 1 = \square\ - 5 = \square\ - 2 = \square$

6. $9 - 2 = \square\ - 2 = \square\ - 2 = \square$

7. $12 - 6 = \square\ - 1 = \square\ - 2 = \square$

Critical Thinking Skills

Math Investigations

Blast Off! Write the facts from the chart on the rocket, counting down to blast off!

20 − 10 = 10
___ − ___ = 9
___ − ___ = 8
___ − ___ = 7
___ − ___ = 6
___ − ___ = 5
___ − ___ = 4
___ − ___ = 3
___ − ___ = 2
___ − ___ = 1
___ − ___ = 0

Blast Off!

12 − 5
1 − 0   10 − 2   5 − 3   8 − 4
20 − 10   7 − 1   9 − 4   6 − 3
11 − 2   0 − 0

Math Investigations

Critical Thinking Skills

Complete each subtraction wheel.

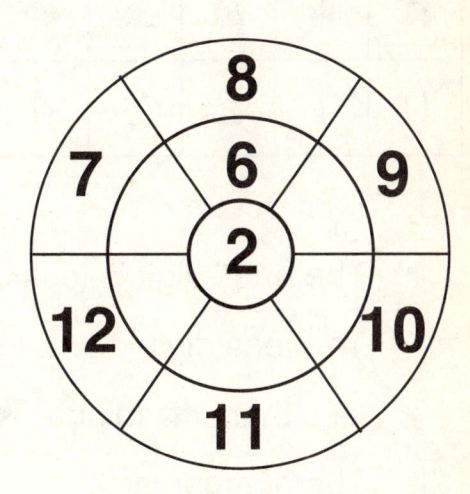

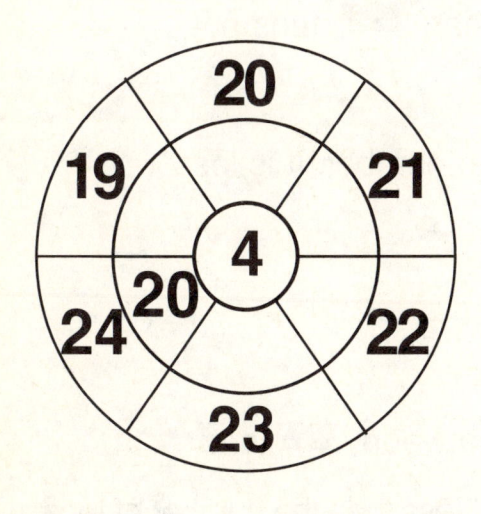

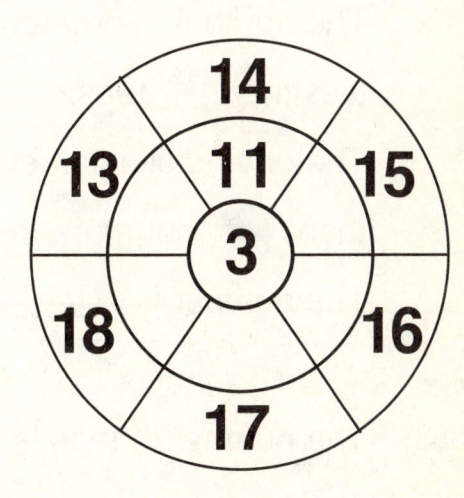

Wheel 1 (center 1): outer 2, 3, 4, 5, 6, 1; middle 0

Wheel 2 (center 2): outer 8, 9, 10, 11, 12, 7; middle 6

Wheel 3 (center 4): outer 20, 21, 22, 23, 24, 19; middle 20

Wheel 4 (center 3): outer 14, 15, 16, 17, 18, 13; middle 11

Critical Thinking Skills

Math Investigations

Read the clues. Use the pictures to find the secret number. Write and draw the number.

✖	★	■	▲	●	▬	◢	▱	♣	✺
0	1	2	3	4	5	6	7	8	9

1. I am odd.

   The ones digit is less than ▲.

   The tens digit is greater than ✖ but less than ▲ minus ★.

   The number is _____ .

2. The number is greater than ▱ tens but less than ✺ tens.

   The ones digit is an even number. It is less than ▬ but more than ▲.

   The number is _____ .

3. The number of tens is between ◢ and ♣.

   The number of ones is ★ less than the number of tens.

   The number is _____ .

Math Investigations

Critical Thinking Skills

You will need 2 beans or buttons. You will need a dice. Work with a partner. Take turns. Put your bean or button on Start. Pretend you each have $1.00 to start the game. Throw the dice. Move that many spaces. Who gets to keep the most money?

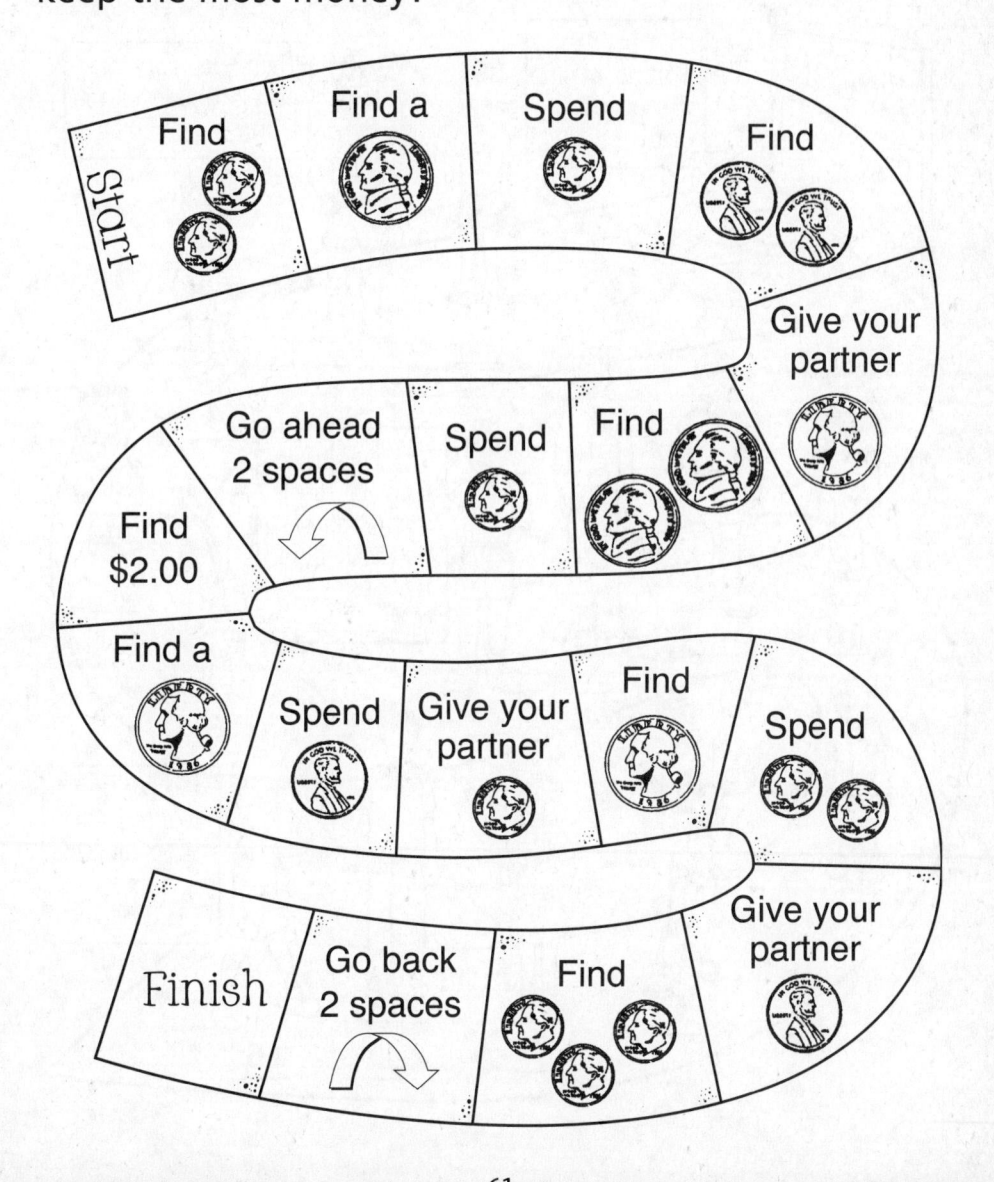

Start → Find → Find a → Spend → Find → Give your partner → Find → Spend → Go ahead 2 spaces → Find $2.00 → Find a → Spend → Give your partner → Find → Spend → Give your partner → Find → Go back 2 spaces → Finish

Critical Thinking Skills

Math Investigations

15 people are in line to get tickets. They are standing in order. Fill in the missing numbers. Write the ordinal numbers to complete what people are saying.

I have been waiting in line the longest. I am _____.

There are two people ahead of me. I am _____.

The person in front of me is sixth. The two people behind me are _____ and _____.

I have been waiting the least amount of time. I am _____.

Math Investigations

Copy this page. Cut the cards out and color them. Use the cards to write subtraction problems.

Example: [∴ •] 2 − 1 = 1

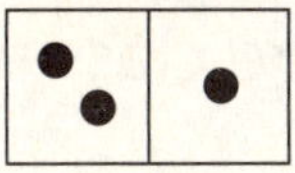

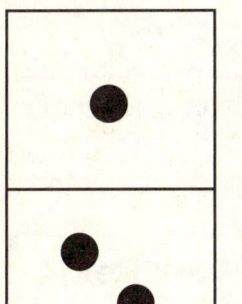

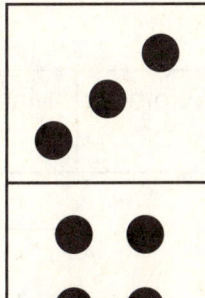

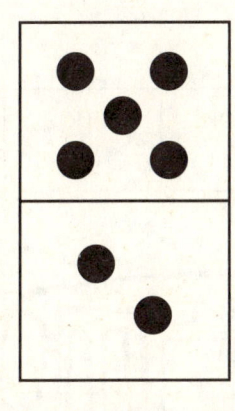

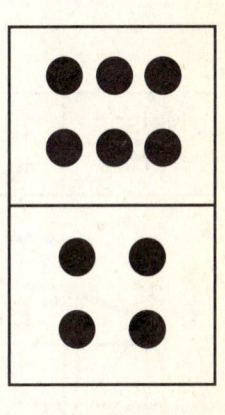

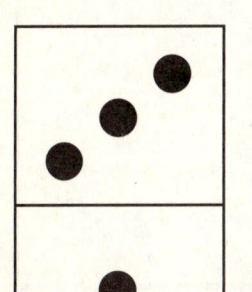

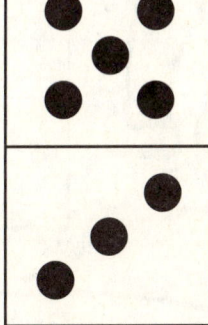

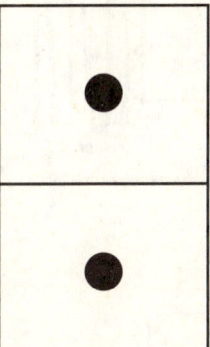

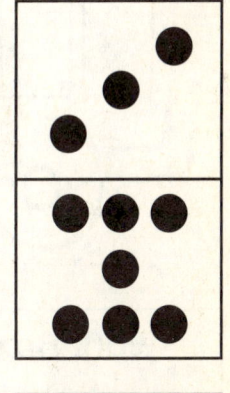

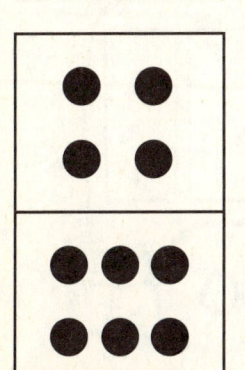

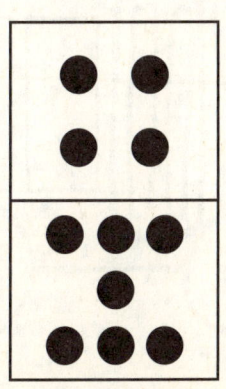

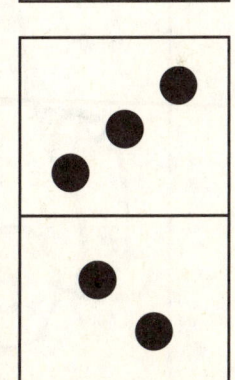

Critical Thinking Skills

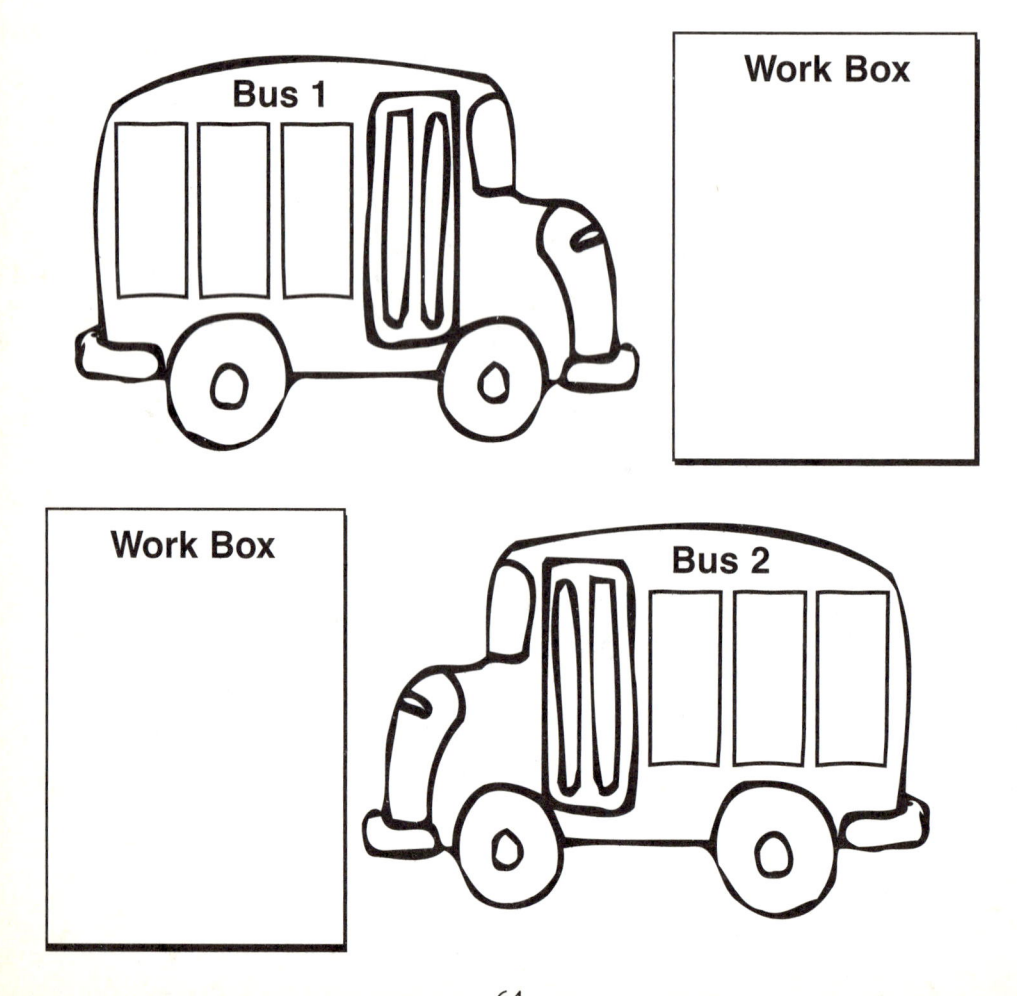

Math Investigations

Six classes are on a field trip to the zoo. They took two buses. Each bus holds 62 children. Add or subtract to find out which classes rode together. Write the class name in each window on the bus.

| Nelson 16 | Arnold 19 | Riggs 20 | Winters 22 | Madson 23 | McCarty 24 |

Bus 1

Work Box

Work Box

Bus 2

Math Investigations

Critical Thinking Skills

Our class played kickball against our parents.

- There are 22 children in the class.
- 55 parents came to the game.
- 22 parents came to play the game.
- 30 parents wore sunglasses.
- 20 parents wore caps.
- 10 people wore blue T-shirts
- 15 people wore orange T-shirts.

Work Box

1. How many parents did not wear sunglasses? _____
2. How many people did not wear blue T-shirts? _____
3. How many people wore T-shirts? _____
4. How many people did not wear caps? _____
5. How many parents did not play kickball? _____

Draw a picture of what you would wear if you were playing kickball.

Brain Teasers

Brain Teasers

Looking for Patterns
Look at each pattern. Draw what comes next.

1. What comes next?

2. What comes next?

3. What comes next?

4. What comes next?

5. What comes next?

6. What comes next?

Brain Teasers

Brain Teasers

Maze
The crab got lost in the sand castle. Can you help him find his way out?

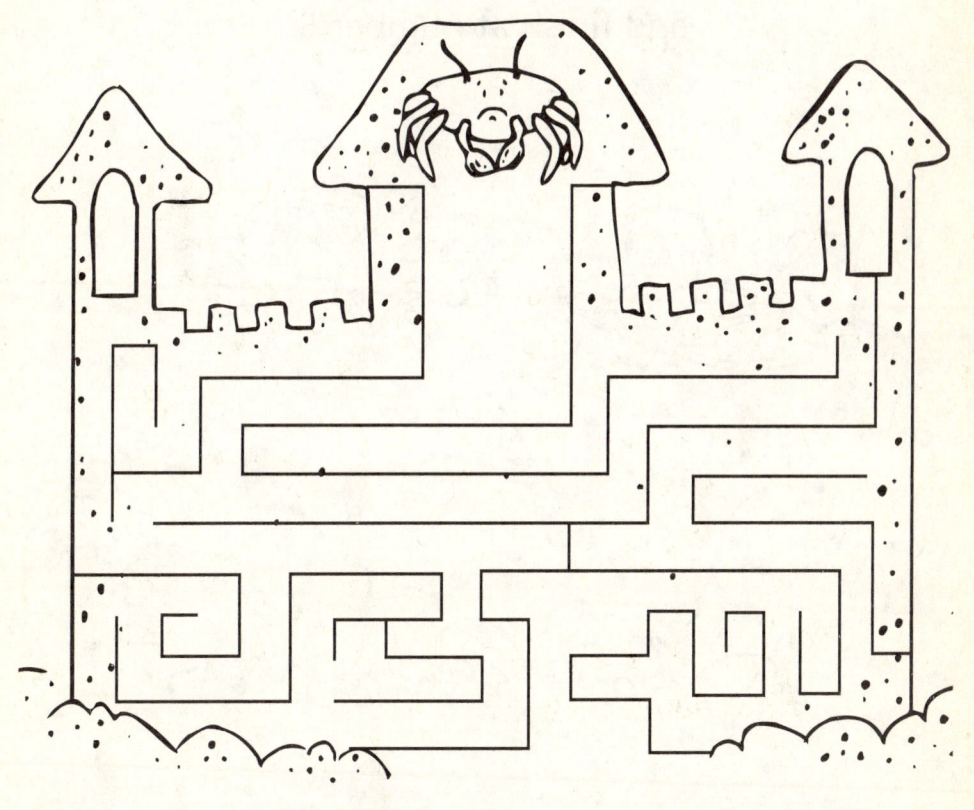

Factoid!
In 1999, 1,650 students built a sand castle that was over 6 miles long!

Brain Teasers

Brain Teasers

Backwards Dot-to-Dot

Connect the dots. Start at number 20, and finish at number 5.

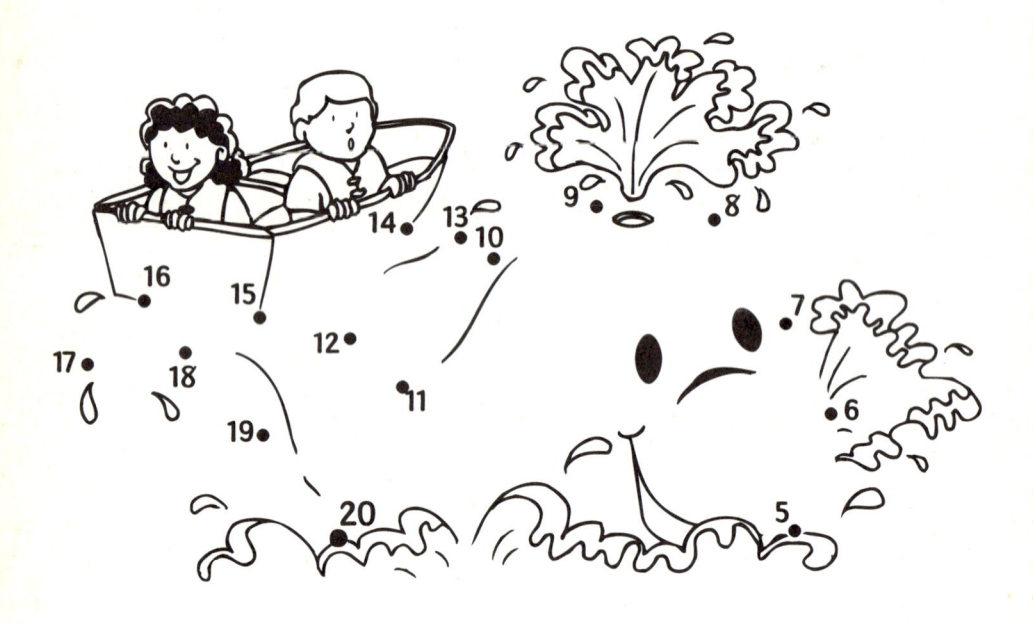

Now color your picture!

Brain Teasers

Brain Teasers

Problem Solving

On which palm will the seagull land? Solve the equation on the tree trunk to find the correct answer. Color in the correct palm branch.

Numbers on palm branches: 3, 10, 9, 8

Equations on tree trunk:
- 12 - 3 =
- _ - 2 =
- _ - 4 =

Factoid!

Question: Is the coconut really a nut?

Answer: No. It is really a fruit of the coconut palm tree.

Brain Teasers

Brain Teasers

Picture Problem: Part 1

Help Rob find all the starfish hidden in the picture below.

How many starfish are there? _____

Brain Teasers

Brain Teasers

Picture Problem: Part 2

If Rob gave Allie 5 of the starfish he found, how many starfish would he have left? _____

If he gave 2 more away, how many starfish would Rob have? _____

Brain Teasers

Brain Teasers

Frog Follies

Answer the questions below.

1. There were 8 frogs in the pond. 2 frogs jumped out. How many frogs were left in the pond?

   _____ − _____ = _____

2. After the first 2 frogs jumped out, another 3 left the pond. How many frogs are still left in the pond?

   _____ − _____ = _____

Factoid!
The smallest frog in the world is only 1/2 an inch long. The largest frog in the world is 12 inches long.

Brain Teasers

Brain Teasers

Color by Numbers

Color all the shapes with a difference of 2 green, 3 blue, 5 yellow, and 7 brown.

12-9
6-3
4-2
12-7
5-3
9-6
12-5
9-2
5-3
11-6
6-4
7-4
8-6
4-2
7-2
12-10
6-3

Subtraction Grade 1—RBP3497

Brain Teasers

Brain Teasers

Fishing Fables

Who catches the fish?

Rob   Allie   Tanner

Factoid!
In 1908, fisherman Joe Muchiowsky caught a 280–pound sturgeon fish. It almost sank the boat!

Answer Pages

Page 5

five	six
four	twelve
eight	seven
two	zero
nine	one
ten	six
three	eleven

Page 6

19, 18, 16, 14, 13, 12
11, 9, 8, 7, 6, 3, 2

Page 7

1. 7
2. 5
3. 2

Page 8

1. eight
2. eleven
3. three
4. eleven
5. two
6. nine
7. six
8. four
9. zero
10. six

Page 9

1. two
2. eight
3. one and three
4. eleven
5. one
6. seven and nine
7. eight
8. three
9. eleven
10. three
11. nine
12. twelve
13. eight and ten
14. four

Page 10

1. $3 - 1 = 2$
2. $2 - 1 = 1$
3. $3 - 2 = 1$
4. $6 - 3 = 3$
5. $2 - 0 = 2$
6. $6 - 5 = 1$

Page 11

1. 1
2. 4
3. 1
4. 4

Page 12

1. 2
2. 4
3. 5
4. 3

Page 13

1. 4
2. 2
3. 3
4. 2
5. 0
6. 4
7. 3
8. 0
9. 1

Seven shells will be colored in.

Page 14

1. 1, 2
2. 4, 0
3. 0, 0
4. 2, 3
5. 2, 1
6. 0, 1

Page 15

1. 4, 1, 0, 1, 2
2. 0, 3, 4, 1, 0
3. 6, 2, 0, 4, 3
4. 2, 5, 5, 3, 2

Page 16

1. $2 - 1 = 1$
2. $6 - 4 = 2$
3. $6 - 0 = 6$
4. $5 - 2 = 3$

Page 17

1. 2, 0, 1, 3, 4
2. 1, 4, 2, 0, 2
3. 0, 3, 1, 5, 4
4. 2, 0, 1, 4, 0
5. 2, 2, 3, 1, 3

Page 18

1. 4–four
2. 5–five
3. 3–three
4. 2–two

Page 19

1. $\begin{array}{r} 4 \\ -1 \\ \hline 3 \end{array}$
2. $\begin{array}{r} 5 \\ -2 \\ \hline 3 \end{array}$
3. $\begin{array}{r} 3 \\ -2 \\ \hline 1 \end{array}$
4. $\begin{array}{r} 2 \\ -1 \\ \hline 1 \end{array}$

Subtraction Grade 1—RBP3497

Answer Pages

Page 20
1. 7 − 4 = 3
2. 9 − 2 = 7
3. 11 − 5 = 6
4. 8 − 3 = 5
5. 10 − 5 = 5
6. 12 − 4 = 8

Page 21
1. 12 − 6 = 6
2. 11 − 7 = 4
3. 10 − 6 = 4
4. 12 − 2 = 10

Page 22

1.
9 − 1 = 7
10 − 3 = 8
11 − 9 = 3
7 − 4 = 2

2.
11 − 4 = 3
8 − 4 = 1
12 − 9 = 7
7 − 6 = 4

3.
9 − 9 = 7
11 − 6 = 2
7 − 0 = 0
12 − 10 = 5

4.
10 − 9 = 2
8 − 6 = 1
12 − 0 = 4
11 − 7 = 12

5.
7 − 2 =
10 − 10 = 5
12 − 3 = 0
9 − 7 = 9

6.
10 − 4 = 6
10 − 6 = 3
8 − 5 = 9
9 − 0 = 4

Page 23
1. 7
2. 3
3. 2
4. 7
5. 2
6. 2
7. 9
8. 2
9. 9

Page 24
1. 3
2. 3
3. 4
4. 10
5. 0
6. 3
7. 3
8. 7
9. 6

Page 25
1. ⑧, 9, ⑧, 11
2. ⑩, 0, ⑩, ⑩
3. 0, ④, ④, 6
4. ⑤, ⑤, ⑤, 7

Page 26
1. 12 − 4 = 8
2. 7 − 5 = 2
3. 9 − 4 = 5
4. 12 − 6 = 6
5. 8 − 2 = 6
6. 10 − 3 = 7

Page 27
1. 5
2. 4
3. 1
4. 2
5. 3; hidden crab
6. 2

Page 28
1. 4, 8, 0, 8, 3
2. 6, 2, 4, 0, 9
3. 5, 5, 7, 5, 5
4. 6, 0, 2, 1, 7

Page 29
1. 4, 1, 11, 2, 2
2. 3, 12, 9, 6, 6
3. 4, 7, 5, 11, 2
4. 4, 7, 7, 9, 6

Page 30
1. 3
2. 6
3. 8
4. 2

Page 31
1. 1 ten, 2 ones
2. 1 ten, 4 ones
3. 1 ten, 3 ones
4. 1 ten, 0 ones

Page 32
1. 1 ten, 7 ones
2. 1 ten, 3 ones
3. 1 ten, 5 ones
4. 1 ten, 9 ones

Page 33
2, 3, 10, 12, 6, 9, 0, 8, 4, 11

Page 34
1. 41, 9, 95
2. 30, 37, 19
3. 39, 17, 13
4. 65, 15, 89
5. 79, 6, 26

Answer Pages

Page 35
1. 15 − 5 = 10
2. 14 − 7 = 7
3. 17 − 8 = 9
4. 16 − 5 = 11
5. 18 − 13 = 5
6. 13 − 9 = 4

Page 36
1. ④, ④, 7, ④
2. 0, ⑩, 15, ⑩
3. 3, ⓪, 15, ⓪
4. ①, 2, ①, ①

Page 37
1. 12, 4, 10, 11, 7
2. 0, 12, 12, ⑥, ⑥
3. ⑥, 9, 13, 3, 0
4. ⑥, 17, 8, 8, 12
5. 7, 9, 18, 10, 11

Page 38
1. ⑨, 12, 2, 16, ⑨
2. ⑥, 14, 16, ⑥, 3
3. ⑤, 11, ⑤, 12, 7
4. 8, ⑬, ⑬, 4, 1
5. ③, ①, ①, ③, 5

Page 39

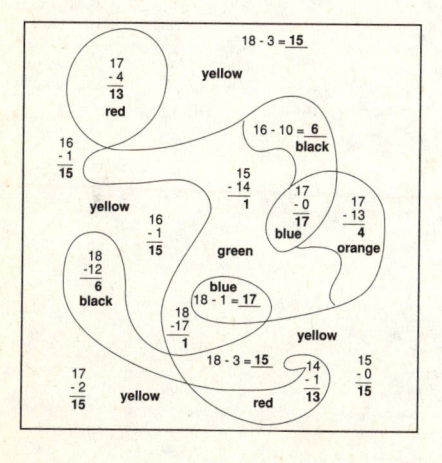

(coloring/maze answer key image)

Page 40
1. 6, 14, 8, 9, 1
2. 8, 6, 9, 13, 3
3. 5, 5, 10, 1, 0
4. 8, 6, 5, 7, 8
5. 12, 6, 11, 10, 5

Page 41
1. 5, 7, 15, 7, 13
2. 12, 1, 8, 6, 2
3. 3, 7, 10, 14, 2
4. 12, 10, 12, 13, 3
5. 15, 7, 4, 4, 2
6. 17, 12, 15, 5, 2

Page 43
1. 5   2. 2
3. 5   4. 5
5. 2   6. 2, 1

Page 44
1. 10, 14, 4, 3, 18
2. 1, 16, 16, 12, 14
3. 13, 0, 14, 16, 1
4. 11, 13, 16, 2, 0
5. 0, 12, 0, 11, 1
6. 2, 11, 15, 9, 17

Page 45
1. 8   2. 16   3. 27   4. 18

Page 46
1. 18¢ − 9¢ = 9¢
2. 15¢ − 4¢ = 11¢
3. 16¢ − 8¢ = 8¢
4. 17¢ − 9¢ = 8

Answer Pages

Page 47
1. 2, 1, 1, 2, 1
2. 2, 7, 1, 1, 0
3. 1, 10, 2, 5, 7
4. 3, 0, 3, 4, 0
5. 3, 8, 3, 9, 0

Page 48
1. 1, 0, 4, 6, 0
2. 5, 5, 11, 2, 4
3. 0, 8, 8, 4, 4
4. 3, 1, 4, 4, 7

Page 49
1. 6, 2, 12, 0
2. 0, 4, 13, 8
3. 2, 1, 5, 6
4. 6, 3, 3, 1
5. 4, 14, 5, 9

Page 50
1. 7 tens, 4 ones
2. 9 tens, 6 ones
3. 43
4. 78
5. 100
6. 3 tens, 3 ones
7. 5 tens, 0 ones
8. 26
9. 52
10. 3 tens, 8 ones
11. 4 tens, 9 ones
12. 66
13. 35
14. 10 tens, 0 ones

Page 51
1. 26, 27, 11, 20, 20
2. 0, 2, 25, 22, 26
3. 69, 0, 11, 77, 45
4. 10, 28, 24, 30, 71
5. 22, 21, 24, 7, 33

Page 52

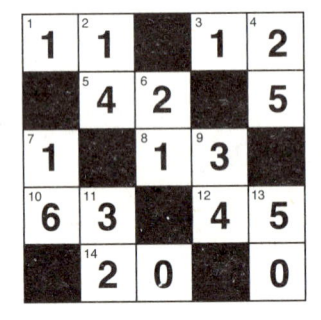

1	2		3	4
1	1		1	2
	5	6		
	4	2		5
7		8	9	
1		1	3	
10	11		12	13
6	3		4	5
	14			
	2	0		0

Page 53

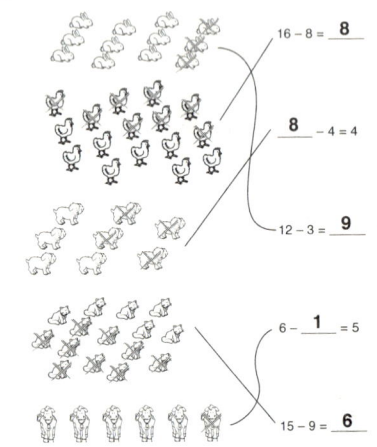

16 − 8 = **8**

8 − 4 = 4

12 − 3 = **9**

6 − **1** = 5

15 − 9 = **6**

Answer Pages

Page 55

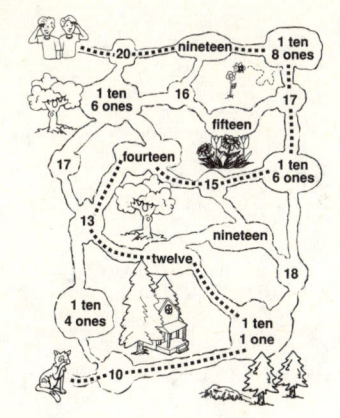

Page 56

Page 57
1. 8, 4, 2   2. 9, 6, 5   3. 13, 5, 2
4. 8, 6, 5   5. 9, 4, 2   6. 7, 5, 3
7. 6, 5, 3

Page 58

11 – 2	10 – 2	12 – 5	7 – 1
9 – 4	8 – 4	6 – 3	5 – 3
1 – 0	0 – 0		

Page 59

Page 60
1. 11   2. 84   3. 76

Page 62
1. first, third, eighth, ninth, fifteenth

Page 64
Bus 1
Nelson 16; Winters 22; McCarty 24
Bus 2
Arnold 19; Riggs 20; Madson 23

Page 65
1. 25 parents   2. 67 people
3. 25 people   4. 57 people
5. 33 parents

Page 66
1.   2.   3.
4.   5.   6.

Answer Pages

Page 67

Page 68

Allie and Tanner are on the tail of a whale!

Page 69

The seagull will land on the palm branch with the number 3 on it. That branch should be colored.

Page 70

There are 12 starfish.

Page 71

Rob would have 7 starfish after giving 5 to Allie. He would have 5 left after losing 2 more.

Page 72

1. $8 - 2 = 6$
2. $6 - 3 = 3$

Page 73

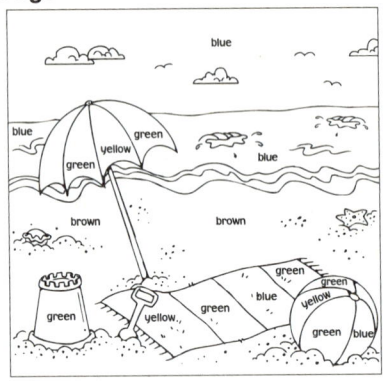

Page 74

Allie catches the fish!